Through A Glass, Finally

by Joyce Jacobson

ISBN: 979-8-218-22885-9

Cover photo by: MaLija
Design and Layout by: Peg Rivard

*For my mother and father
who finally saw me.*

Acknowledgements

With loving thanks to Barbara Haber, June Gould, Ruth Steinberg, Toni Farkas and Mary Sochet, the women in my writing group whose support and wisdom were instrumental in the creation of this book. Their vision helped me get my words out into the world.

June Gould, remarkable teacher in whose class many of these poems were written; Ruth Steinberg added her expertise and facilitated the production of this book; Barbara Haber for the exceptional photography and to Peg Rivard for her amazing technical skills.

Some of the poems in this collection, some in earlier versions, first appeared in the following publications, anthologies, and on-line sites:

Jewish Women's Literary Annual (2005 and 2006), Advanced Writer's Retreat,(2010,2012,2013,2014) The Poets Roundtable – Anthology (2007), Decolonizing Poetry: Hyphenated Americans, Poems from 84th Street A chapbook Anthology, Beyond The Margins by June Gould, The Journal of Psycho History, Gallery And Studios Art Journal (online).

Table of Contents

Chapter 8   How They Have Endured the Heat

Chapter 9   If This Then What

Chapter 10 We Are Done Doing Our Duty

Preface

Water: A Fluid Path

As a child I walked in the rain
to feel its chill, its moist tickle,
the taste of frost on my tongue.
Drenched I went home
singing a wet tune
until scolded by my parents
something about clothes clinging, hair soaked,
the cold, the cold, the cold.

Then there was the sea I tiptoed into
starting at the edge.
The current pulled, waves smacked,
jellyfish led the way deeper into the freeze.
I was in love with all the colors.
Sky touched the top of the ocean's pulsing breast.
Teen years filled with lust in the movement of waves
stirring me, stirring me, stirring me.

I took roads to the river
to listen to its rushing words and respond.
It told me the bark on the trees gave their approval,
leaves that floated downstream said yes,
pebbles at the periphery applauded my path.
The current carried me
to the left, to the left, always to the left.

Chapter 1

IT COULD HAVE BEEN OTHERWISE

It Could Have Been Otherwise

If my mother at 16
had not met my father
on the Coney Island boardwalk
in Brooklyn on a summer's day
with the sun streaking
her short brown hair blonde
my father's hair
wavy thick and dark
his moustache not filled out
her thin curvy figure
sitting on a blue square box
where they argued about
the radio the music selected
if my mother had not gotten her way
to hear Artie Shaw play Nightmare
I might have become a squirrel

I'm Sorry I Was Late

I saw a speck of light
as I grappled with the umbilical cord
tightening round my neck.
Peculiar prongs poked me.
I pulled back, but my tiny hands
slipped along your sides.

I'm sorry I was late.
People in white masks scared me.
Why couldn't they leave me where I was?
I could hear your heartbeat,
wiggle my toes to the tune.
Everything was soft and warm.

I didn't know I was late
until they slapped me,
passed me from one to the other,
punished me, put me
in a noisy dorm in a bright lit crib.
All I wanted was a room of my own.
No pink ribbons, just rainbows
on the horizon outside my window.

The Kitchen

I sat in an infant swing – gray cotton fabric
with two openings for chunky legs.
I swung in the doorway to the kitchen,
watched my family as they watched me,
all brown eyes, brown, brown and brown.
I saw the square wooden table
that squeezed in five
when my grandmother ate with us.

Meals were served on proper plates
with appropriate meat or dairy silverware.
When I could reach the handles
on the white cabinet drawers
filled with forks, spoons, ladles,
I tried to memorize
which spoon went with what.
But I never understood.

Alone at the table with a shiny tablecloth,
I had to finish everything piled high in my dish.
I moved food from one end of my plate to the other,
mashing it, thinning it out
letting it fall off in tiny pieces.
I wanted to throw the food into the garbage,
out the window or down the drain.
But I could not – lying was a sin.
My tongue would burst with blemishes.

Perhaps a smaller portion
or a choice of vegetables
not those green and red uglies.
Then maybe I would not
have to sit alone in the kitchen
with the blue and white linoleum.
and the sink that was always so clean.

War in My House

American flags wave
at the entranceway
to my apartment house,
in front of Hymie's candy store
and the Lincoln Place deli.

My father is in our living room
in a soldier's uniform.
He holds a funny looking hat
in his hands, pressed tightly against him.

I see the sharpness of his knuckles,
I want to open them, hold his hand
as I do when we go to the park,
he plays handball
before he puts me on a swing and pushes.

I look up toward his face
looking for the perfect white teeth,
his smile, his laugh.
It isn't there as he hugs my mother.
Why don't they pick me up
if they are going to dance?

Strange that my grandmother sits
in the other room, the door closed,
my brother is on the couch,
not outside playing ball,
even the radio is off.

Who is crying?
No, I won't say goodbye.
Where is he going? I want to go.

Sometimes I fight too.
Mostly I am a good girl.
War, I know about War.
Let's play War or Go Fish.

Things I Never Knew

Why can't I speak as my father carries me home
promising me ice cream and stories? Why do we have
tonsils if they need to be removed? What else does not
work in my body? I open my mouth, nothing happens.
How long will I be speechless? May I have chocolate
fudge that swirls in the plate as it melts?

Why do I never do anything right? Did they know I
poured the milk back into the container without spilling
a drop? Why can't I play at the open window with bugs
from the trees while my mother sleeps late on rainy
days that add to her depression?

Why does my grandmother, who sleeps in the room
with my brother and me, speak Yiddish so well? When
I am old, will I forget English and speak only Yiddish
like all the old ladies on the block?

Why am I always wrong and fail to please my mother?
What made her throw the new lace handkerchiefs back
at me and tell me to buy something for myself but never
for her? Why didn't I cry? They didn't hear me anyway,
except for my grandmother who holds me from time to
time and speaks the language I was afraid to
understand. Why did I never learn the tongue they
used when they didn't want me to hear their secrets?
Why did I never speak my truth? Why did I lose my
voice?

Red White and Blue

In Brooklyn on a block
with stone stoops and marble hallways
old ladies sit on wooden benches,
speak in many tongues,
a homeland here, a ghetto there.

Words scream about stories of bloody bandages,
trains going miles through snow and sleet.
They whisper about numbers and raw flesh,
turn away from me, from my street,
from my Spauldine
that hits the penny on the line.

These women stare into each other's pain.
They do not look at speeding skates,
how quickly I can stop.
They do not hear me yell: "free for all"
from my hiding place between low cut bushes
in front of my apartment house.

Women with gray hair,
faces lined deep with fear,
huddle to talk of news from far away.
They sit and wring their reddened hands.
I put on my tap-dancing shoes and sing.
This is my street, my block.

You are here I want to yell,
away from the ashes of your homeland.
You are here on my turf
in my boundary
on my red, white and blue.

Michael

I was four when I held Michael's hand.
He said we were engaged.
A photo shows me in a winter hat,
hands in a furry muff,
kissing this boy next door.
Together we raced through streets,
roller skated down the hill;
my skate key around my neck,
his in his pocket.
We played punch ball, king, queen,
hit the penny.
On weekends his mother bought us
hot-dogs with sauerkraut.
Michael punched my arm.
He really loved me.

One day Michael was not home.
My shouts under his window
went unanswered.
I sat on our bench.
He did not show up.
I brought my favorite marbles
to trade with him at the oak tree
where our game began.
He was not there.
I knocked on his door,
rang his bell,
screamed his name
as loud as I could.
No one opened his door,
windows were shut tight.
Neighbors were silent.

Forever crept by
before Michael came home,
his arm in a sling,
his hair cut short,
he did not smile.
My parents whispered to me,
neighbors called me aside to talk.
Polio, what is polio?

In Those Days

Heat rose through my window
spread itself around my bed,
dampened my hair, my forehead,
the sheet beneath me.
I woke with enthusiasm
looked out at the street,
the park beyond it,
the sewers that became
first and third base.
I dressed quickly in shorts,
a tee-shirt, sneakers and white socks.
Games happened in those days –
stickball, ringolevio, kick the can.
Sweat meant movement,
running to catch the ball,
skipping in boxes marked in white chalk.
It meant days off,
no more pencils, no more books.
Ice cream wagons with popsicles
that sweetened the tongue,
ice chipped from a block of ice
on the back of a truck
to spread around your neck, your face
or to suck until gone.
It was Brooklyn in summer.
Streets sizzling with childhood;
in those days it was home.

Excerpts of My Life in Digits

The shaking of one finger from those I love
to reprimand me and not just once.

Thumbs up for actions I took and more often
didn't take as I perfected procrastination.

The daintiness of my pinky when I drank English tea,
sipped hot sake or slugged shots of scotch.

All five held high to give me more time
to drink, dream, play solitaire.

A higher five to congratulate me
for a fine job if ever I would finish.

Scolding from the whole hand pushed the wind
into my face with a slap. I closed my eyes.

A special finger for a ring to bind me to another
which I never wore but saved for children I never had.

Digits flexed in unison a simple motion of goodbye,
the exhale of waves, when everyone leaves.

Fingertips touch fingertips to talk to heaven,
ask for forgiveness. I press hard!

Apartment 3A

I wish I could say
I closed the door to my own room.
It was never my room. It was our room:
my brother, my grandmother and me.
No locks were allowed on any door
except the tiny white bathroom
and that one could be opened with a table knife.

I had to account for my whereabouts
in the four-room apartment.
Where was I? What was I doing?
Was it something constructive?
my mother would ask
from her bedroom
behind closed double doors.

Sitting at the window watching neighbors,
boys on bikes, cars and buses
was my idea of constructive:
being tuned in to some other world
right outside.

I was not cleaning the room,
putting my clothes away,
washing dishes in the sink.
I felt the cool Brooklyn air
on my inquisitive, young face.

I observed leaves and ladybugs
on the windowsill,
women on parkway benches talking loudly
about Poland, Roosevelt, the price of eggs.

My mother called out asking
Where was I? What was I doing?
Was it something constructive?

If only I could close my door and lock it.
If only it was my own room.

Smokin'

I sit on a stoop across from my school.
The fence around the yard is rusted and black.

It is cold and dirty on the steps
covered with cigarette butts and burnt out matches.

We pass loosies to one another,
cigarettes bought at Harry's candy store,

two for a penny, short and white,
stuffed with dark tobacco.

Paper sticks to my lips, I drag on it then pass to Sandra
who sucks the tip, makes it light up and burn.

She inhales deeply without a cough.
I watch in awe and ask excitedly

"How do you do that?" She blows smoke
from her mouth, some through her nose.

She gives the cigarette to me. I look around,
no teachers, no students outside Marshall Jr. High.

I hold it between thumb and forefinger the way I think
Marlene Dietrich does but it is more like John Wayne.

I inhale; watch the fiery end flame,
devour the paper, sizzle up toward my fingers.

I will not cough; I will not choke.
At twelve I am grown up.

I take a drag, exhale long streams of smoke,
flick an ash, tap it to the ground.

I loosen my ponytail, shake my head.
My long, dark hair falls to my shoulders.

I lean back against the steps on the stoop
feeling sultry and star bound.

I Threw My First Book of Poems
into the closet on the top shelf,

wrapped in my grandmother's Yiddish paper,
The Forward.

I took it from the living room couch
where she left it.

Everyone was working
somewhere out there in Brooklyn.

My brother delivered liquor, carried heavy boxes
to people in the neighborhood.

Mother was downtown, a salesgirl at A&S,
a department store that sold the best custard.

My father drove to a factory, he stood
most of the day cutting leather, thick and soft.

My grandmother worked in a factory
where she made gray and white feather dusters

attached to oak colored sticks.
She never let me visit there.

At night when lights were out,
I wrote about what I did not understand,

scribbled on yellow paper or white scraps,
hid the words in my closet

where they silently aged.

Chapter 2

REMEMBER ME, I AM MEMORY

Mother's Dream

My mother dreamed of adventure.
She walked among
the past and the northeast
to roll between mountains,
wash her dishes in the sea
behind hollow clouds
of monotony.

Her sleep was tender
with breath that could have
perfumed hotel rooms
until she spent her affections
on a stoop in Williamsburg.

Time shifted her course –
words became loud,
belched fire
beyond the wildest
of her illusions.

Strain and sweat swept her away
from the magic carpet
rolled in a thick clump
beneath her fleshy bottom.

She sat on misdiagnosed secrets.
Aspirin became her favorite flower,
sniffed and inhaled
with all the aromas
she chose to live in.

My Father's Career

My father worked in a sweat shop –
stood ten hours a day,
leaned over a massive machine
to cut thick pieces of leather
then trimmed them
using a sharp curved blade.

In his dark colored work pants,
his torn tee-shirt wet with sweat,
he made parts of shoes and handbags,
piled them high to be counted
so he could be paid pennies per piece.

On days off he sang and laughed,
played handball at the park,
pushed my swing,
sat when I played barber,
danced with my mother
to the tunes of Glenn Miller.

After fifty-five years
of seasonal factory labor,
he decided to retire at sixty-seven.
His back, permanently bent,
could take no more pressure
from the pounding of cutting machines.

On his last day of work,
his boss showed his appreciation
with a box of chocolates
(milk chocolate and caramel).

Reconstructing My Brother

In the corner of the room
where I once played
are items necessary
to reconstruct my brother
from the top down.

I use earth colors
except for those that are not.
Brown twigs and a bird's nest,
a plastic comb stuck in the middle
of auburn hair copied from mother.

An arm from a phonograph,
makes melodious moods.
There is a radio, a clarinet, a saxophone.
Through windows at the Palladium
I see him mambo, cha cha, lindy.

I chop down a sturdy tree trunk,
mold strong muscles for tennis and golf.
Roots, thick and grainy dig deep,
eliminate the pain in his leg.

I carve his shoes out of crystals,
cut from boulders near the sea,
I dunk him in salt water
not once but twice.

His nose, a snail's shell,
inhales and exhales through reeds
that are his mouth.
He swims from Beach 24 to Beach 26.

Marbles that he looks through
cast from salt across the street
tinted in reds, yellows and blues
colors clear vision.

He gathers up his trophies
with ceramic fingers curled enough to throw a ball.
I paint him with affection from childhood,
soak him in memories, strong but filtered.

Memories I need to remember.

Sugar Cube

My grandmother drinks coffee,
dunks thick sugar lumps into it,
sucks the cube to her delight.
I watch, envious of her tasting
that sweet moist flavor.
She gives me one rectangular lump to dip
into her glass of coffee.
I dip once then twice, it changes color.
My parents complain
as they watch from the doorway.
I look into my grandmother's eyes,
the same dark brown as mine
that smile and approve.
She touches my hand
"Ignore them," she whispers in the Yiddish
I do not understand but read through her eyes
or the touch of her fingers.
She speaks words of endearment.
I watch her face,
wrinkles at the edge of her eyes,
olive-colored skin just like mine
except for some marks on her cheeks,
her private signs of age.
We open my first-grade book, read to each other,
learn the words and pronunciations
my mother teaches us.
It is our book with the blue cover, thick, yellow letters
and stains I made from wet sugar cubes.
She laughs, kisses me –
her lips, soft and pale against her dark skin.
We share her coffee, my book, our sweet tooth.
We understand each other
we speak the same language.

Immigrant Grandmother

I never knew
your given name,
or why you changed it.
The trip across the sea
not an easy one
for a sixteen-year old girl
or were you twelve or thirteen?
We guessed your age –picked a day to celebrate
as long as it was not the thirteenth.
Why did that scare you?
What happened when you were thirteen
or on some thirteenth day?
Was it thirteen steps you took,
thirteen the number of your house,
the number of the ship
that brought you elsewhere
cold and afraid?
You ignored that number,
looked away from it,
passed that feeling to your children
and your children's children.

American years passed.
At your funeral
I learned your given name-Malka.
You were eighty-five or seven or so
and you were buried on the thirteenth.

This Poem Begins

when my mother wakes,
lights a Camel cigarette,
brews coffee,
speaks of her dead father
who came to her in a dream
which means something awful
is going to happen.
He sends complex, dark signals
without a hint of where to look,
who will be affected.

Mother ponders:
Will her husband who sits slumped
on the couch
remember her tomorrow?
Now he knows she is his wife.
But do they have children?
He thanks her for the bread
she did not give him.
He hums, he sings
a show tune, a popular song,
once, twice, twenty-six times-
always the first line, only the first line.

He asks if it is time to go to sleep.
His eyes dull, his sight poor.
She answers as she bites her lip –
tells him in a weak whisper
they just got up.
He stands but does not straighten,
his back is round and bent.

He wants something to eat.
He will sit at the table.

She asks what he wants.
"Don't bother." my father tells her:
"I am not hungry."
He turns, heads toward the door.
"Where are you going?"
"I am going home," my father says,
"I am hungry".

Women in My Family

on my maternal side had voices
that were always raised.
Chatter shook light bulbs,
men's inner ears,
children could not
run fast enough
or far enough away.
Doors slammed, roofs shook,
the fire-escape
clung to its hinges.
Delicate female hands
were fleshy, some chunky,
some dipped in chicken fat.
Music from clanging pans
accompanied their tart alarms:
"Sing before breakfast and
you'll cry the rest of the day."
The women in my family
told stories,
tales of things past
somewhere on the streets of Brooklyn.
Faces flushed with anger,
frustration, steam from soup pots.
Lips painted with lipstick
or Vaseline
as words were chosen
with the bite of piercing barbs.
Years passed like winter storms,
their thunder turned to rain,
a soft drizzle.

A Touch of Color

We crave the comfort of color.
The gray of my mother's hair
in the soothing, beige painted room
of her own speaks to us.
She sleeps a deep sapphire sleep,
legs hanging over the brown bed frame
to keep her heart pumping crimson
through internal pathways,
some open, some clogged.
Peace settles on her pale face-
crinkled leaves with dark and light veins.
Dimples dip deep into her flesh,
lines zigzag around mouth and eyes
like the baked crust of a cherry pie.
Awake she smiles through murky shades of memories
dripping into yellow fuzz of a life forgotten.
There is acceptance in the ginger blaze of sun
on treetops – snow white, plush green
as she looks out the window,
a colorless window that no longer opens.

Time Stopped

when my father asked me
where I lived and if I was married.
I looked into his eyes to find him
among the ticking of clocks.
Watered down,
he was watered down.
I knew he loved me, he told me so
even without saying my name.
He knew, he absolutely knew
I was someone important in his life-
maybe a friend or a daughter.

Time stopped when my mother told me
they were talking about her-
saying she was married to an American
but he was elsewhere.
He was on her dresser
between a silver frame and a hard backing.
Did she remember that he passed away?
She remembered me – introduced me
over and over as her daughter,
never saying my name.
She knew where she was.
She was in a small room
near the nurse's station where the pills were,
where voices spilled over into her room

Time stopped when my brother
did not meet me on my mother's birthday.
He got lost he told me,
he was finally home.
Now he knows my voice when I call.

I am still his baby sister. He says my name.
I cannot ask him questions
about what he did today, what he ate.
It makes him angry.
He tells me he does not know what he did.
Then he tells me over and over again.

I am clutching time, holding it close.

Remember Me, I Am Memory

I, memory, stick myself to every strand
and bit of foam
in your father's pencil-drawn mind.
Intruders, cruel and slick,
squeeze through
to close crevices in your old man's
field of recollections.
He sees a snowflake
but doesn't know
where it came from.
A piece of lettuce
on a plate confuses him.
He knows the color green
that covers the ground
but what is the ground?

Once he danced
until claws clutched his ankles.
Music lodged in remembrances
when he sang a tune from long ago
where he now lives
among shattered thoughts
he cannot pronounce.
Family photographs float
through his open spaces.
Clouds cover me, memory, with shade.
I pass that on to your father.
There is less light.

Still he sings a song.
He sings it again and again and again.
There is nothing I can do.

I Was Not There

My mother's gray sweats
and sweatshirt
lay on the lady's chair,
creased, pinched, half folded
like my thoughts, my memories.

My mother died this February,
the 19th, a Sunday morning.
I was in a deep sleep
when the call came,
when dreams got wiped away,
when my tears were stuck.

I was not there
at the nursing home.
Not that day
or the day before.

I thought she would eat again,
sip the cool cranberry juice
from the thin plastic container,
dip her fork into mashed potatoes,
pureed meatloaf with smashed carrots,
wipe her mouth on both sides
with the long bib around her neck
then nibble the Dunkin Donuts
I would bring

whenever I was there.

Letter from My Grandmother

Can you believe
there are clouds in heaven
above us and below?
The sea is everywhere
you want it to be.
Sand is cool beneath your feet
if you just think about it.
My collection of shells is endless
with a sprinkle of sea glass.
I sit in the shade of any tree
and read my newspaper
which tells of good deeds –
birth, commitment and death.
They speak all languages here
and no matter what it is
I understand.
My cooking is better than ever.
My potato kugel
has won me golden wings.
Tea up here is the very best.
I sip it now and then
from a tall glass
as I look out my window
from my favorite winged chair.
I no longer add jelly to hot water.
Sugar cubes are plentiful.
There are no hospitals here.
Yes, doctors and nurses –
who never take
your blood or even your temperature.
But no need,
I have not been sick in thirty years.
There is always a card game

on one cloud or another.
My best game is still pinochle.
I win all the time.
Here comes my husband.
We take walks in the forest
and on city streets.
Keep thinking of me.

Regards from your father.

Chapter 3

THE WOUND

The Wound

I rub the same wound.
It bleeds, never heals.
I cover it with gauze,
conceal it.
It festers.
I buy potions.
Plead with druggists,
doctors, analysts.
It opens again,
slightly healed
or so it seems.
It oozes familiar patterns –
droplets of red and the blues.
I am desperate to mend it,
disinfect the germs,
wipe away dried blood,
color it flesh and skin.
I whine from the couch I lie on.
There is an attempt to patch it
with therapeutic theories,
bathe it with oils,
seal it with a new hide.
If allowed,
the scab would fall off naturally.
I could move at my own pace
flawed, scarred but functional.

Great Expectations

Today *hope* you would be as old as I.
      Once you were bold and accessible
      but you left me along the way
      with newscasts, words whispered incoherently
      and a path that caused my soles to bleed.

Your tinseled tongue told me about
      places to play-- sandboxes, gardens with flowers
      every color of my crayons.
      You brought me to a sandy beach
      to rest my head, taught me to look up
      and blink back at the stars.

I embraced what you led me to believe
      through tales you told.
      You held my hand in classrooms
      heard my prayers
      to remember two times six is twelve.
      You pointed to the sun to remind me of a new day
      before night stuffed it in its pocket.

I danced in my prom dress,
      reached high to grab the prize--
      expectations you held by the tail
      and swung high above me.
      My dance partner kept me balanced.
      Then the music stopped.

I busied myself with love, life and complications,
      too weary to wait for you.
      Rain washed away my weathered home,
      hurricanes smacked me.
      I felt like a lonely limb, clinging.

Still I long for you, *hope,*
        my thoughts twisted with fantasy.
        Now you come in a bottle
        with a narrow top,
        a package of pills stuffed with cotton.

I Empty Myself

Flush all out
in a deluge of tears,
burst open the dam of clutter,
send salt that stings
back to its sea.

I empty myself.
Write lists,
untie all nots
that blot blank paper,
unpack days jammed one into the other.

I pry open the crux of me,
remove band-aids
so blood can flow
and feelings rush free.

I empty myself
from head to toe
from lung to breath,
wander through words of uncertainty
and clouds of camouflage.

I empty myself
pull weeds of deception,
liberate thoughts
that clog my consciousness.

I stretch my capacity,
strike a vital tone of harmony;
reconcile all those many parts of me.
If I empty myself.

My Angry Other

I come home wanting to touch
and soothe my angry other
who stomps on the blood red rug
unraveling with every step.
I speak softly to ease
her clenched fists,
the twisted lines of a face
that appears to melt
into fires of rage.
I walk towards myself,
wipe the tears from our eyes,
talk of ordinary times
that can be smooth as water,
quench my thirst,
cleanse my hands,
cool the heat
that burns between us.

Labyrinth

Patches of grass,
snipped short here, long there
struggle against my footsteps.
Clover huddles in corners.
Leaves browning with goodbyes
scatter above weeds and wild flowers.
Slate sits over some green, smothers it,
creates a path for travelers – I walk it.
An odd shaped branch,
thick, scaled and broken
lies over mounds of bald earth.
Dried limbs point in different directions
like small fingers fidgeting.
One faces the hardened earth
another lies naked without its bark.

Grass in the labyrinth flattens
like a living room rug –
guides me, the visitor,
round and round.
Frail plants create order
in tiny rows of color.
I follow another path –
let it take me through its winter green.
Wind and trees whisper
that I can go either way.
I won't go back to the beginning.
I move to the center of it all
to rest and reflect
on the back of a decorated stone slab
held up by nibbling stone squirrels
who might tell me the right way to go.

Life Is A Good Thing

I told you life is a good thing
when I pulled you out of the raging sea
that thrashed your body
east and west then let go.
You washed up on pale sand
your face grainy and wet,
breath barely audible.
"Stand up!" I shouted.
You got to your knees,
I pulled the rest of the way
until your feet stood firm
on ground you tried to lose.

I tell you life is a good thing-
tear off the wrapper, step out,
wear colored ribbons in your hair,
walk in new places, leave footprints,
find silhouettes that speak to you,
taste the intensity of light,
walk between shadows,
hold an infant with a toothless smile,
touch her bulbous cheeks,
applaud the woman dancing
with an old partner, a new partner,
one she doesn't know.

There is an ocean of promise -
jump into it.

I Called on You

I prayed for a sister
who would play with me,
teach me the alphabet
and explain why white clouds
form animals and faces.
    I received a doll with blue eyes,
    long lashes and hair I could not comb.

I knelt before the opened window,
of my apartment and whispered
that I wanted a car to drive downtown
to shops, great movie houses
with crowds of well-dressed people.
    My father put a pink ribbon on my brother's
    old bike and passed it down to me.

I talked about love among friends,
old neighbors and co-workers
searching for a common view
and why I was inside out.
I looked up for a response, the way everyone does.
    The silence terrified me,
    I stepped deeper into shadows, waited for word.

From the temples and churches, I asked:
"Who is watching the world?"
I raised my voice
pleaded for shelter for the homeless,
serum for the sick, food for the famished.
    The hush cut like thorns
    inflamed my fury.

I shouted against war, raised a fist,
set blame on stars at night that watch us,
rays of the sun that touch us,
and a moon that lulls us to sleep, to forget
about answers we wait for.
      "Do something!" I screamed, and it echoed back.
      "Do something!" and finally I understood.

Chapter 4

THE PATH OF BLACK AND BLUE

Breaking Ranks

I come from a long line
of heterosexuals –
one man, one woman
and so forth and so on.

Here I am –
same skin as my grandmother,
olive with a hint of beauty marks.

My dark eyes reflect
my father's and my maternal grandmother's.
But I see things differently –

for me the world moves to the left,
on the fringes or downtown
into the shadows of a stone wall.

My mother steps into sunlight,
removes her apron,
wears a feathered hat with fur.
I prefer a purple cap.

No lace handkerchiefs for me
like my mother, her mother
and their mothers before them.

They walk one behind the other
on hard earth
holding each other's hands-
their paths cemented.

Me?
I walk on roads still rough and gutted.

An Outstanding Love Poem

I stand on tiptoe
at the threshold
of a wide-open door
painted plum purple.
A tempting fruit-stand
stands inside,
a standard wood-cart
of oak and pine.
The vendor stands tall, majestic,
black liquid hair
drapes over her shoulders,
untangled, soft, free.

She stands for courage.
I stand still, stare.
She blends apples and pears
from the garden.
Flames from her oven spit sparks.
"Stand back!" she shouts.
Layers of love spill into her pie pan,
a light-colored crust round and flaky.

I taste. I understand.
Even behind closed doors
we do not stand a chance.

The "F" Word in the '70's

We found Feminism in back alley bars —
The Dutchess on Seventh Avenue,
a dark, dreary place
filled with women.
In this shady space,
we expressed ourselves,
stood straight and proud,
longed to break barriers.
Some lived lives of lies,
detached, imprisoned –
hiding who they were,
disguising their strengths and intellects.
The "F" word brought us permission
to move closer to who we were,
who we could be.

But how far would they let us go?

From Lesbos to Cappuccino

It might have been 30,000 years ago
when we felt the cold
and warmed ourselves with fur
from another.
In the dark, open mouthed dwelling
we huddled, shared our fears,
spoke few words,
communicated with our eyes
and the speed of our fingers.

Now in this time
you touch me, I tense,
sip my cappuccino,
look to see if anyone noticed.
We sit rigid in a
low-lit Starbucks
waiting for the restaurant
next door to call our name
so we can dine on beef and oysters.
We sneak gazes at each other-
melt our fleshy armor.

In the cave feelings drip
and spread like rain water
splashing on the river bank.
You touch me without restraint.
I respond with ease.
We mimic the beasts
that roam within our view.

Here in this world
the waiter takes our order
shifts his eyes
to our hands that touch.
His face cold,
turns with disgust.
Diners stare,
sizzling with fantasies.

We eat our tenderness
and stiffen to the chill.

Would You Come Back

to the house with columns
you ran away from,
the father who fed you booze
then promised money
if his little girl stayed home?

Would you come back to the bars
where you spilled your sweat,
women turned away,
some offered open arms
at last call?

For the door you broke open
to talk to an old flame;
police locked your wrists in cuffs
and the key cost you
when daddy heard?

For the fights from trucks
you jumped off,
a bottle of booze in hand,
the other arm got broken,
lipstick was applied
to your swollen lips?

For the ten dollars you got
to give blood
then spent at a dirty saloon
where people disliked you
because of the way you looked?

Would you come back
to those back rooms
where women danced with you
when you bought them drinks,
took you home and loved you?

For the poems you wrote
on brown paper bags
you stuffed in your pocket
next to the empty pack of cigarettes
that you shed tears to get?

For the bail daddy paid
from his thick checkbook
kept in his expensive desk
behind the walls of his mansion
that he asked you to leave?

For the rehabs you were sent to
after imaginary bugs
drove you crazy
as you huddled in the corner
of someone's bed?

For the miles you fled
with a strange woman
after you climbed out the window
during bed check and left the therapist
a half note, half poetic explanation?

For the drunken trip you took
from a California mountain
as you drove into the sea
from high above?

Would you really want to come back?

American Pie

Her indifference sits on the table,
in an old, cracked bowl.
She mixes in raisins and racism
until thickened with intolerance.

A photo of needy children
flashes across the T.V. screen.
She turns away,
hums a lullaby.

She peels the red skin off apples,
slices the white flesh
into a well-oiled dish,
adds her grandmother's recipe-
a little of this, a little of that.

With moistened fingers,
spreads the mix
as her mother did before her
to bake American pie
with the same inflexible flavoring.

Back in The Seventies

we did not hold hands
when we walked in the streets
whether in soft sun or hard rain.
There were no rainbows then
no open spaces to fly like birds.
I would not put my arm around her back.
I might risk my wellbeing, my life.

We walked together but   apart
as if people were watching,
measuring the distance between us,
reading the love in our posture,
our glances at one another.

I wore heels more feminine than loafers.
She wore open toed sandals.

Surreal Painting in Words

In this bar, men line
the road to hell
with a winning hand
of four aces.
Some dance to maracas
beside orange flames.
A she-cat, sultry
and inviting
looks away smiling,
claws outstretched,
her nipples point left and right.
A jubilant skeleton
with bones delicate and fine
adores her,
tiptoes towards her
in rhythm and song,
decadent.

Trees stand
adorned as wood stained boxes.
The devil wears a smile
as twisted as his tail.
His spiral shaped penis
hangs between thighs
shaped like a mule's.
Observe this canvas –
how it dares to spill
its sinful song
and tempt all creatures
with wine tinted oils
of a colorful hell,
a painted hell,
hell.

On the Fringes

At the tavern men whisper
about her curves.
She fills the space with sensuality,
beauty applauded with loaves of lust.

Barstools are empty
except mine and hers beside me.
Fragrant perfume delights.
Fabric from her blouse touches my arm.

She turns towards me.
Her eyes smoky grey
with dark lashes.
A smile on her lips.

I smile back,
lean in closer
to talk about weather,
rain, the chill in the air.

We look at each other with familiarity.
Thoughts blend into a silent song –
a lovely melody,
lyrics will follow.

My words pause in midair
when a man leans over,
whispers in her ear.
Air grows thick between us.

I inhale deeply,
clutch my drink and drink,
tap my fingers on the bar,
force myself to look away.

Stonewalled Tales

Once a woman lay with a man, resented it, smothered tears in her pillow, cursed her marriage vows, but never left his house.

Once a woman followed her husband's instructions, added a woman to their bed, embraced her as her husband did, left with the beautiful stranger until the stranger left her.

Once a woman was athletic, played basketball well, walked with a mannish gait, had short hair and rough hands. No one hired her.

Once a woman left her husband, fell in love with a woman, was hated by her daughter. Never saw her child again.

Once a woman camped in the Adirondacks with her female lover. They cooked on the outdoor grill, kissed in the privacy of their tent, were shot by a hunter who stalked them.

Once a woman held a woman's hand, walked the avenue at dusk, hospitalized at dawn, beaten by a gang of men.

Once a woman covered her breasts with tape, wore jeans with a fly front, a man-tailored shirt and was raped because of it.

Once a woman loved another woman and died for it.

Once a woman partnered with a woman, never allowed anyone else to know.

Once a woman whose husband was wealthy, hired a maid, she had someone to love.

Once a woman told her father of her true self, he told her to leave, sat shiva for her.

Once a woman loved a woman, felt shame and homophobia. She led a lonely life.

Once a woman nurtured her daughter, mothered her with care, kissed her every day, learned the girl was different, abandoned her.

Once a woman told her twin she was gay. "I'd rather you be dead", the sister said.

The Door Speaks

I am a deep purple painted,
weather-beaten, wooden door.
When the sun comes up,
I keep the rays out,
stay still until street lights light.

No one knocks to enter.
I slam shut after each woman,
clothed in camouflage, walks through.
Music beats shatter bits of my frame.
Behind me drums, bass,
floorboards vibrate.

Women sit at dim corners of the bar,
or in low padded seats of a booth.
There is talk, laughter, dancing –
and they touch.
Some look frantically
around the room.

Late at night, they slip out past me,
rush anonymously in denim, silk and uneasiness.
I watch them leave –
two by two, one by one.
It is like this every third Thursday
when women can meet.

Some return home to empty rooms.
Some tiptoe past parents.
Some go back to husbands
or find love in another's bed.
Some fight fists smashing their identities
leaving deep purple bruises.

Imaginary Twin

I was invited into my mother's life.
My twin had to find her own way –
elsewhere
along dirt roads in Midwest farmland
where she cuddled with cows,
kept a pig as a pet.

I attended high school,
more to socialize than learn,
she packed her papers,
moved abroad to study human nature,
art and poetry.

I walked to the subway
squeezed in among
other office workers.
She held up signs in Alabama,
marched with a mighty few
carrying a flag of peace and inclusion.

I wept in discos and bars
for want of one person,
who was waiting for someone else.
My twin married once but could not call it that.
She went to Washington in 1999
to wait for equality
where she grew old

waiting.

Pray for Them

Hidden in the shadows
behind masters of masks,
a man waits to step into sunlight,
tighten the buckle of his belt,
stand tall, walk among crowds,
tip his hat, bow from the waist,
flick an unsightly cigar ash.
He wants to be called sir, mister or
simply man as he flips a coin in the air
and whistles through his teeth.

This man by becoming himself
singes the eyes of his brothers,
fists clench tightly against him.
He grips his mother's heart
with his small, strong hands
causes her tears to spill.
She curses the belly that warmed him
through her own blood.
She pollutes the air around her
with hateful words, repulsive thoughts
and denial of her motherhood.

The man who fathered him
left years ago
before a new shape was formed –
when flesh peeled from flesh,
bones splintered and were repaired.
His father turned away,
left, took his pride with him –
no forwarding address.

They left him alone, eclipsed

in the darkness where priests ignored him,
rabbis shunned him.
Storekeepers turned him away,
neighbors stared and threw trash.
What happened to the parents who loved him
when he was Daddy's little girl
and Mama's sweet angel doll?

Who Killed Me?

I found myself dead on the carpet.
My mask split open like a wide horizon.
I searched the crevices of darkness
for a clue.

Birds scattered like splinters,
flew through cracks in the windows.
My footprints made no impression,
no one would know I was hungry.
My hair was darker than I realized,
I wanted to see it blend
into the floral pattern on the rug.

Had I died of natural causes?
Would anyone worry about that except me?
There were no traces of bites
only tiny touches of poison.
My arms lay rigid at my sides, cowardly.

A pencil stuck out from behind my ear,
the fine point of an accountant
examining minutia.
Bosses with fat wallets
looked down at me
maybe I just forgot to salute.

Next Time
I want to be
a dot on a domino set,
deep and decorative.

I will eat roses and lilacs
with a gravy of dirt,
mix berries with a hair dryer –
cool, safe, plugged in.

I will break eggs,
make my own omelet
with peppered words,
salt from healthy seas.

There will be a proper noun
to present on a platter,
commas carved from cherry stems,
a side of small letters and capitals.

When I come back,
I want to bathe
in a fruit salad,
mix it up,

return as the buttons
on someone's blouse,
row myself down Main street,
Broadway or the Coney Island surf.

What I mean when I walk
on slices of purple onion
is let's do it over.

Chapter 5

WRITE AWAY
RIGHT AWAY

Write Out Loud

I will ease myself
out of homophobia,
walk with Lesbian Pride.
There I spoke
the word aloud.
The ground is intact.
My face is not in flames.
Angels still dust my path.

I permit myself
to tell truth
through poetry.
The symbolic door unlocks,
I open it, cut
the cord of self-censorship.

Passion defrosts my words
once stiff and unfaithful.
No more tripping
over weathered chains.
It is time to stand up straight
and write myself out of the closet.

Write Away

I had no idea the gate I stepped through
led to the large house on the pointed hill,
red brick smothered in sea weed,
windows the shape of vowels.
Pale faces peered through cellophane coverings,
steps made of glass, cracked and fused
by the heat of the sun that never went down.

A woman in bright white greeted me at the door,
took my hand, led me to the room of the living.
Books, formed like sofas
and high-backed Victorian chairs
as comfortable as the plain oatmeal blouse
I wore when the ketchup dried.

I licked my fingers, shook hands
with aides, nurses, men in grey suits.
We talked about what happened yesterday,
why I needed a room.
I unpacked my papers, spread them around
on table tops and computer keys.
Poems from A to J were clipped together
near the window sill where birds in tiny aprons
closed the drapes.
From K to Z were placed
on the bed that would be mine.

Night tables held lamps with bright yellow bulbs.
Drawers were filled with eyeglasses
as were shelves above the bed.
I would not have a roommate.
The woman next door
left a wall of pencils outside her room.

Her door knob was a giant eraser.
How I envied that.

The aide assigned to me read.
I sat in a chair.
Her words were sharp and clear
until I could not hear them anymore.
She stood in a bucket of coffee
to let the caffeine rise.
She read and read and read.

A woman in a white uniform
gave me a lined legal pad.
She put words in my mouth.
The taste was bittersweet.
I swallowed the entire paragraph,
choked on her commas.

My door had no lock.
People walked in the hallway,
some carried their own chapters in black and blue.
Poems were red, notebooks yellowed.
I saw a blonde woman and a fair haired man
exchange semicolons.

A woman who walked in circles
whispered words with W's.
I watched her mouth and wondered
would I wind up that way?
Bells rang, people recited prayers,
poems and eulogies.
I followed the crowd.
It was the write thing to do
write away, right away.

Well, It Is Done

My wounds grow deep.
I threaten to perform my own surgery
with pen in hand on white paper,
paisley bed sheets or a freshly painted corridor.

Morphine kicks in at the end of the verse,
the poem, the story telling.
Words stuck in a haze of anesthesia,
hide behind bright lights
in the operating room.
Blood flows.

Accidents happen
like a slip of the tongue
or the sling of outrageous vocabulary
grip the pulse of punctuation.
Arteries get stretched,
passages are on the mend,
the blockage removed.

The poet awakens
her final piece of work heals.

I Swallow Words

I swallow my own words,
letters in large chunks.
My expression is telling.
I gasp, utter indecent sounds,
choke them back
before anyone hears.

I chew letters in seconds,
hear them crunch.
I spit out the I's and U's
rinse the A's with vodka, gin or ginger-ale,
flush away the taste.

Vowels leave me
with my mouth open.
My hands reach
for the bread and butter of words,
small letters, capital letters
spread and sliced in layers
devoured by simple sentences or paragraphs.

Then the spice,
apostrophes and commas
to slow the process down
while I grab a p o e and m
in case the characters are thrown away
with the garbage and scraps
before I can consume them.

About My Hands

My hands flex on computer keys,
occasionally grip an old ball point.
Fingertips glide over the smooth keyboard
circle letters of the alphabet.
I stop to scratch my head,
smooth my hair down on one side.
There is nothing to write about.

From hunger and thirst,
I grip a bottle of orange juice,
touch the tip of the glass to my lips,
hold the tumbler steady.
I cover my eyes with my hands
listen to the silence,
wait for words, thoughts, images.
Still nothing to write about.

As a baby I sucked my thumb
for comfort, not the right but the left.
Later I could tell left from right
as I summoned that infant in me.
In school my digits served as calculator
passing me from one math class to the next.
During recess I gripped a ball, threw it far,
applauded myself for the skill.
It was nothing to write about.

I observe my hands once sturdy and strong
now spotted and veined like the root of a tree.
Still they clench and open,
wipe my messy mouth,
scratch an itch with satisfaction,
brush away tears
because there is nothing to write.

Fingers, once graceful and long
matured crooked and dry.
Knuckles protrude, bulge
like lumps on the head of a cauliflower.
Even the fortune in my palms,
misguided by the onslaught of
superfluous lines and crevices,
has nothing to say.

I Write This Poem

In my room, dark and littered,
I count piles of paper on the desk
beneath the window.
I sit in a large chair,
lean on worn wooden arms.

I press my glasses close to my eyes,
read from my batch of poems,
tear several pages, toss them one by one
on top of bits of blank paper
in a waste basket already filled.

Dozens of pens stand, their caps off –
once moistened tips of color,
blue, black, red,
dried up, clotted.

A tray beside me holds a plate
of day-old rye with roast beef.
I drink from a glass of iced tea –
drops drip from its stem
smear the words,
stain the paper,
soil my thoughts.

I sit forward in my chair,
look out the window,
my breath slow and even,
my imagination oddly stirred.

I write this poem.

She Is A Poet

who finds the ending of a poem
like a bulb in a nightlight
that shows the way
through shadows of its own.

Her house is a place of dreams
with silver screens and broad windows
that look out upon
a road, a detour but no stop sign.

She is touched by trains, tree trunks,
icicles before they melt;
feels sorrow and humor in words,
photographs and the multicolor
of cats' eyes.

This poet walks on tiptoe
in alleys, avenues
and highways
to find the beginning of a verse.

Like a robin
who sings in the spring,
she needs to write –
have her words take flight,
to fit peace inside.

She observes
changes in seasons, tides,
sounds of the sea.

She wants to write it all
on yellow paper with blue ink
or red crayon on the wall.

The Pressure of My Pen

Poetry plays with my pen
or does my pen make a point of poetry?
Perhaps it is all about words
winding their way out into the world
where I can watch what I am saying
see the inspiration between the lines
around punctuation at the end, after it happens.

The end of my poem often looks at its beginning
bathing in the rhythm of intention.
It pushes itself around without me
without my conscious what to do
what not to do.

Form, forever out there
whether ink smudges or not
whether the clicks of computer keys
force me to feel trapped
or write about a heart that is broken.

I receive the words
watch them move across the page
pushed by ink creating images.
I enter into my poems, read them,
share them with the objects in my room.

How does the table feel?
What did it say to the question mark?
Did the desk ask to do away with wandering words?
Does lined paper like the pressure of my pen?
And the lamp? Can it turn itself on and off?
Who controls the commas, words before, after?
My words become a completed poem.

I sit at my desk,
tiny ceramic cat statues applaud.
There is no more pressure.

A Women's Café

A women's café –
hot coffee, fat-free muffins,
chamomile tea.
Poetry stokes the fire
applause echoes
through dark beams,
exposed and strong.

A large mike on a make-shift stage,
blackened windows, lights full lit,
air perfumed with feminine sweat.
The pulse of passion pounds
through meter and rhyme:
words too often unspoken.

Poets line up, tea in hand,
clothing draped in layers,
scarves, African headdress.
Ms. Lorde's volcanic voice erupts
From a land where other people live.

Timeless thoughts expressed aloud –
the posture purely feminine.
Words ignite
mothers, wives, sisters,
warriors, feminists, lesbians.

Diving into the wreck –
A Rich exposure of words –
truth, awakening!
Coffee cools –
strong tastes linger.

The torch is passed.

Chapter 6

THROUGH A GLASS, FINALLY

Out of The Shadows

Troubled,
she sat at her bedroom window
writing poetry in the middle of the night
by street light and moonlight
while everyone slept.

She put pain on the page
for review, a word, a resolution,
someone to read her verse,
clarify her theme.

Her pen moved awkwardly on paper;
she could not see the lines.
Letters sloped, words slid into shadows.
When purged, she hid her notebook
under the bed.

She left poetry in the closet
of her own apartment.
She had a job, a bank account,
friends to hang out with
at bars, at every party scene.
Little time was left for poetry.

She wrote when tears felt stuck,
her hands trembled,
sweat flooded her pores.
She scribbled her angst
until exhaustion released her.

Pride opened her eyes,
so she could write in the light of day.
She left text on top of her desk.

Coming out was what it's cracked up to be.

Through A Glass, Finally

My mirror tells two tales.
An image on the left
shows me dressed in blue jeans, sandals,
a colorful shirt falls loosely around me.

The right side displays me
wearing high heels,
tights that fit tightly,
a push-up bra forms deep cleavage.

The image to the left
mirrors hope in my eyes
of my own words, my own choices,
my own....

The right reflection reveals a husband,
children, a large stove,
and an apron
tied around my mouth.

There is a pull to the left
when the right reflects
hair tightly knotted into a twist
and calloused feet that face the wrong way.

Finally, I shatter the looking glass,
fracture the framed copy,
take steps to crush the pieces
into a puzzle I put back together
with my own hands.

Once Upon A Girl

A child I once knew
liked berries on the vine,
tiny and black on crooked stems.
A handful was a palm of stain,
a mouthful, a taste of pleasure.

Elders told the girl
not to eat the fruit
with its pesticides, preservatives
and unwashed hands of strangers.
She frowned and turned away
into spreading fear and obedience.

The youngster felt
a want so sweet
against the sting of higher powers
who whispered distortions in her ear.
She never disobeyed –
wore restraints and shackles
in loops, knots and thick
black and blue wool.

As a woman,
face to face with discontentment,
she stripped her artificial coverings,
strolled among flora and shrubs,
touched the vines,
ate the succulent fruit
and felt approval
from the sun
upon her naked skin.

Acrobat

I shed many skins through the years
tripping over chaos and waste.
Now mirrors reflect a face
I strain to identify
and still say "I am me."

As a girl I climbed a high wooden fence
behind my parents' house,
felt the thrill of accomplishment –
a reprimand iced my pride – an off-season chill.

Dating boys from the temple, the Catskills,
the corner bar,
I dressed in short skirts,
wore heels that pushed me over the edge –
a circus act on a trapeze,
an electric prod in my pocket.

I sipped scotch in dismal bars,
stuffed my fear into double shots.
The bottle offered courage
I heard someone else speak.

A gentle touch awakened a truth in me
when a woman held my hand,
I became me –
no longer a cloud before a summer rain
shifting shape and drifting by.

What I Have Inherited

In the language of my family,
voices raised to the level of rage,
a sun sinking into depression,
expressions spit out in two tongues –
one from the old country
one from the now.
I stood with head bowed
embracing my fear before it turned yellow
like the Cream of Wheat with lumps
I was forced to eat –
because children in Europe were starving.
I learned to eat heartily, devour it all.

I have a first name and a last
but nothing in-between, not even an initial.
Nothing like Mary Jane Sutton,
or Murray Herbert Baum.
I was empty, always missing something
until I realized there was less
to sign on the signature page.

Alcohol had its uses –
fed me courage on the rocks,
encouraged me to dance
as if I were happy,
start up conversations that were meaningless
or sparked an exchange of affection
that led to toasts of *"L'chaim"* and morning coffee.

Time cast its shadow on me,
ticked its tock into my psyche,
pushed me out of the closet,
out from between cocktail dresses,

suits with skirts too long
and frocks I bought but never wore.

Now in this time of acceptable tradition,
men are men and women are women.
Some men look like women.
Women dress like men.
Some women who look like women are men.
Some men who once were women are men.
Some don't care who is who
and then they all fall down.

Someone Loosened Her Restraints

She hid behind dark glasses
to restrict the view.

Her steps were missteps
out of sync at Sunday mass.

When exposure threatened,
fear leaped through her.

Newspapers in bold print
alarmed her consciousness.

Her clothes were knotted,
shoes worn out from running.

The weight of ancestors
cursed her, poured out in tears.

The mixing of pronouns
lost her her job.

They stared at her differences
and jeered at her.

Feelings were masked;
she sulked.

Someone loosened the restraints
from the collar of her nature.

Hiding in the trenches
was no longer an option.

Purple became her favorite color-
she stood with Pride.

A woman knocked on her dreams,
released the lock,

she opened them wide,
and breathed in her own life.

Through No Fault of Her Own

she took the road on the left –

a twisted path with vines and thorns.
She ran

with a broken heart, bent shoulders,
an array of tears.

She stumbled as she crossed
into her own life,

reminding herself to breathe,
to get beyond

the thick layers of impossibility –
to speak her truth, live in the open.

Wobbly feet moved slowly,
until she reached

a congregation of women
and found her own seat.

I Am Not Writing

I am not writing an apology for not writing
or for songs I never sing,
musical notes I never learned to read.
I am not writing to say I love you;
if I did it would be a lie.
I am not writing my profile on Match.com
that too would be a lie.
I am not writing directions to my house,
my phone number or yours.

I am not writing about the Dutchess,
the lesbian bar on Seventh Avenue,
bartenders with short hair
and rolled up sleeves.
I am not writing about women
who sit in the darkest corner,
those who go downstairs for a smoke,
the time I met my teacher
who panicked, told me
she tutored a student there.

I am not writing about the attractive woman
who sat in a wheel chair
months after she jumped off a roof.
I am not writing about the jazz singer
who, I thought,
wandered into the bar by mistake
but knew everyone there.

I'm Going to Carry My Bed

to Times Square
where lights blaze new ads
and marquees shout story lines.
I'm going to set up my fourposter
on the rooftop
beside pigeons, their coop
and a goose down cover,
where Camel cigarettes blow smoke
through a hole in a billboard.
I'll scream: "I'm here!"
wrapped in flannel sheets
tucked in to all my edges
all my corners and all around
the mattress where my body
dumps its fatigue.
My slippers drop on tourists' heads
and I wave.
This is my life
which consumes me
even in sleep.

I'm going to carry my bed
to the heart of the city.
Watch my dreams light up,
reveal the hide of me.
Take note of my two pillows,
one stuffed with feathers
the other with sweaty secrets.
I'll shake them out
above all your transparent heads,
your tight-fitted minds,
your eyes wide with images
I scribble for you.

My mattress is finally dry.
My nightshirt loose and free
holds the wide spread of my body.
I'm going to carry my bed
to center stage
on Forty-Second Street, New York City.
So watch me beat my naked breasts
to the rhythm of who I am.

Lesbian Tea Dance

The sun shines this summer day when Tea Dance
begins. A subtle high stirs the guests. There are singles
and couples and those undeclared.

White is what most women wear. One, an artist, prefers
black on black. Susan, a therapist, stares as she stands
on the side of the dance floor, stomping to the beat of
the drums, lyrics of love lost. Some stand alone
searching for something or someone somewhere.

> Christine tells anyone who listens
> her curly blonde hair
> frizzes from humidity.
> Her tanned face is attractive.
> The reddish-brown brings out
> the green in her eyes.
> Something Denise has noticed
> as she steps closer to her.

Mildred and Roberta hold hands as they have done for
the last six months. Everyone knows, everyone
watches. Judy stands beside them, smells of baby
powder and diapers. She talks of her newborn, looks
into the crowd for familiar faces but especially for those
who are not.

Speakers are loud, dancers hot. Some hoot and holler,
their arms pushing up the invisible sky reaching for
rhythm all around them. "Do you wanna dance?" I hear
someone say to a tall brunette swaying on the
sidelines. Molly is dancing with Cheryl, her ex, the first
time since they split some years ago.

Michelle whispers to Annette as they stand at the bar. Joann walks towards me. I turn away – too late. She touches my hand to greet me. I stop and try not to look into her eyes where I will see wanderlust, candlelit dinners and summers by the sea. I feel her fingers squeeze my flesh; my sunburn heats, its bronze turns red. The white jacket she wears is linen with only two large buttons leading to a V-neck where her necklace dazzles in sapphire blue.

Suddenly the music stops.
I see my partner
standing on the dance floor.
A romantic song starts.
I smile as I step towards her
we dance slow and close.

Sappho Starts A Union

I told women at the bar
Sappho was uniting us
with banners, benefits
and lavender badges –
one member will recognize another.
Holidays will be negotiated
along with huge U-Haul discounts.
Personal leaves available for break-ups,
couples counseling not included.
We will get time and a half,
additional days in our lives,
for the time we had to hide in corners.
Closets will only hold supplies,
shoes and Victoria's Secret underwear.
That too will no longer be a secret.
Out! Out! Victoria!
Lipstick, short skirts
and army boots will be welcome.
It will be an open shop – all inclusive.
No more back rooms.
We will work,
serve anywhere with training
regardless of orientation.
Churches and synagogues
will open their doors.
There will be medical and dental
and some unions will be called marriage.

Chapter 7

FOLDING INTO THE SHEET

Cover Me

Stone passes under my feet.

I hear it sizzle through raindrops.

Traffic lights retch.

Fumes fold with the stench.

I have been here before.

It is not worth coming back to.

Graffiti-worn,

Bricks sulk.

My nose struggles for air.

She left.

Her cigarette is out.

It died in its own ash.

The sink is singing plop.

I am folding into the sheet

Cover me.

Dance with Me

Toe to toe in tight shoes
I fall into your arms.
Cheek to cheek, I sneeze.
We change partners.
I sniff, I puff,
wind round and round
under flashing lights.
You are out of sight.
I think of T.J. Maxx –
if the sale will
continue tomorrow.
I sniff again.
Thank you, little straw.
Why are you wearing wings tonight?
Are those lilacs in your hair
purple and plum?

You inhale the room
with guitars.
Your manners appalling
as you spit out
the a string, the b flat, the g spot.
I laugh when you eat the piano
with all the keys
including the one to my house.
Watch me about to fold.
Catch me. Hold me close.
Dance with me toe to toe,
hip to hip grinding,
cheek to cheek sweating.

Remember, please don't speak;
I don't want to know your name.

Lady of The Village

I dress in all my best –
silver necklaces, earrings,
bright beads, green gems,
the reddest of cloth.
I am looking for gentle touches
and jewels that declare your joy
at seeing me.
You are there among the crowd,
the merchants, prosperous and poor.
Come beside me
share my wealth of dreams.
I see you crouching in the sun.
Look at me
see the soft curl of my hair,
the silkiness of my skin,
eyes brown with lust
and other messages.
Know that within me
is a fragile thread of longing,
knotted and frayed.
Come, know my touch, my scent,
juices that wash through me,
feel my wide opened kisses.
You are smiling, your head tilts
toying with my thoughts.
I see you.

See me.

I Listen

hearing words

that surge from your mouth,

sounds that vibrate

and bounce off walls

in dismal rooms.

I listen

as phrases filter

through channeled ears

to all my chambers.

I listen

hearing all those words

still I wonder what you're saying.

The Plaid Dress

You were my woman in the plaid dress
I picked out the shoes
We danced until all music stopped
You don't sing to me anymore

I picked out the shoes
You were wearing torn stockings
You don't sing to me anymore
I never liked that disco sound

You were wearing torn stockings
I wanted to be somewhere else
I never liked that disco sound
You had too much to drink

Your face was red and sweaty
We danced until all music stopped
I found you standing at the bar
You were my woman in the plaid dress

Love Gets Lost

Love gets lost in shaky ground,
moves towards hedges of lies.
Wish you were here
so I could go elsewhere.

I count buds on my rejection tree –
two are dead, some blossomed.
I cup one, only one, in my hand;
blow hard to make it open.

Love gets lost in dark ponds
where mud splatters,
bonds with soil,
without a trace of caring.

Love gets lost among treetops
where robins sing.
Dear Robby,
I heard your call. I wanted to answer.
Clouds and dishes got in my way.

I love you, I once said.
        You do not, sighed my love.
I have kissed you in the night.
        You never brought me flowers.
Oh, how I love you I yelled.
        Don't yell at me, she cried.

I Know Her

I know that woman walking towards me.
She stares straight ahead,
head held high, posture straight.
Sunglasses cover hazel eyes
that see rivers and fantasy cruises.
I know she carries a bottle of wine
in a paper sack at her side.

She does not see me beyond parked cars
and moving traffic on Bleecker Street.
We are on opposite sides.
Once we turned to each other
at night, in bed, wordlessly caressed,
touched in familiar patterns,
creating sighs and releases.

We said words that were fitting,
held hands, pressed our fingers together
molding the scene into photographs
we hung on the wall
but took distance to look at.

On the street all I need to do is cross over,
shake her from dreams I am not part of,
replace memories she keeps
into which I cannot blend.

I know her well –
her scent soaks me like summer rain,
the touch of her hands,
a gentle imprint in my memory.
I see her lines and curves with my eyes closed.
My eyes are opened now.
I walk to the corner on the next block,
stroll among strangers.

Uncoupling

She took the blue from blueberries
stuffed them in a cobalt-colored jar
with a glass top, a metal spring enclosure.
I objected.
Said I didn't love her anymore.

A white bottle of Clorox sat between us
on a bathmat on the dining room table.
Her eyes turned toward heaven.
She zipped her mouth shut.

We never argued
until the Coney Island parachute stopped dropping.
She was like a free fall who never landed.
Once she took my breath away.
I was fighting to get it back.

Her hair was braided.
I took it personally
with all the not's, the no's
and streaks of lies brushed out.
My truth: I always loved blueberries.

The yolk of her omelet, orange and intact,
was no longer up for discussion.
I felt blue, out of character,
at a loss for no longer loving her.

No words passed across the table,
no apologies, no language of love, no caring.
Loneliness was left as the centerpiece.
I don't love you, I said
looking into her eyes the color of seawater.

Dawning

Nightfall and full moon,
thousands of stars,
the city is silent.
Her bedroom windows face water –
a river with a streak on its back.

Our voices hushed.
Hot summer sighs spent.
The scent of perfume fades.
Caresses cease.
Our bodies damp.

She sleeps beside me
on wrinkled sheets, no cover.
There is a smell of burnt candles.
Small flames still flicker.

She dreams, I keep watch
over my misgivings
hold them present,
think about my needs,
my doubts.

The rising sun
greets me with light
through uncovered windows.
Trucks and horns growl,
tires squeal, people yell.

Pigeons coo on cue.
Soundlessly I dress,
join the city at dawn.

The door locks behind me.

Emmy And Me

I think of motels by the sea,
vodka exploding beside ice cubes –
like wrinkled faces smiling.
Moody music spreads across the bar.
We ignore the dust, the eyes of lonely people,
hold hands laughing, really afraid of it all
though no one knew or so we thought.
We help each other out into the storm,
reflect on weighted times we share like pennies
as we hold one another to stand upright
to see the sun that has to peek
through all those clouds.
We take turns being encouraging –
atheists preaching religion in pitched tents.
We drift like the houseboat we never lived on,
bury anxieties with foam and shells
of outrageous days –
including the one
when you left.

The Sink and I

You are the type that looks best
in cobalt marble,
elegant and shapely.
Your metal legs thin and lean,
spread as you put all your weight upon them.
I touch your spotless white, wet edges,
sleek and firm.
That is part of your attraction.
When I get down and dirty
into your rounded triangle,
wide enough and deep enough
for my hands,
you wait for me
to squeeze tiny bubbles of suds,
foaming with fragrance
into your drain.
I can close or open you.
You are willing to go either way.
I wash away the dust of my carousing.
Dirt clings to me.
I rub harder.
With heavy gurgling,
you swallow my filth
and lighten my load.
I caress your knobs.
You become cold then hot.
I turn you on more forcefully.
You flow with a steady stream.
I grab and fondle you
this way and that
until you shut down
because you know there have been
sinks before you

and there will be others to follow,
pink porcelain, milky marble, stainless steel,
older with age spots and stains,
young ones that gush, spray
and tinkle.
It excites me
that others wait for my touch –
because I have always known
you are hung up on the tile wall.

K.O.

I see her face

carved out of liquid distortions.

Bitterness melts into soft lines.

Eyes slip into mine.

My hands wage war

against caresses –

the exploration of her seams.

My dream asks for the night.

Her touch talks to me

through private channels.

She teases my flesh,

dabbles in the traffic of my mind.

I read the silence

on her taut lips

as she tries to taste me

like the beer beside her.

In the high of artificial closeness

her drunkenness fractures my fantasy.

When Words Are Spent

There is nothing to say
when all the words
have been spent.
I listen to the lull.
I scream,
drawing breath
from the depth of my frustration.
You cover your ears
with headphones,
turn inward
towards a drone you can relate to.

I am background noise,
too loud,
too monotone,
to interfere
in your line of fire.
You take aim
with your arched mouth,
shoot me
with your tongue,
peel edges
off my thoughts,
bombard my reality.
My words drop to the ground,
wounded,
you stomp them
into silence.

Sweet Life

Sweet life isn't peas and spinach and broccoli rabe.
It's not that green or yellow that stirs my pudding.
I am not the wash the dishes, clean the sink
take out the garbage kinda gal.
Each year I go to chocolate carnivals, tapioca tastings
and sugar Sundays that indulge and gratify me.

I do not dress up in black veiled hats,
khaki combat boots or heavy holsters on my hips.
No guns to shoot my prey
or prayers to justify bitterness.
It's all dark chocolate, marshmallow centers
and wet walnuts
that keep me on my course.

My road is filled with gingerbread houses, gingerbread
men, women and children with pink frosting
spread across their mouths, crumbs on their fingers
and hot fudge smudge smiles.

This year was a crisis
when greedy forces burned the cakes
and caused cupboards to be bare.
Saltines replaced sundaes,
whipped cream was a mere memory.

Wrappers of Milky Way bars and Baby Ruths
floated downstream,
waste in the harbor where ships stood guard.
Sailors forgot the taste of caramel
and chocolate covered nuts.
On land were cries for popcorn cooked in oil.

My dream is filled with baklava, apple pie, crème
brulee, hamantash, sweet sticky rice,
canoles, honey cake
all served at one table
with a sturdy multi-colored cloth.

Dear President, Prime Minister, Monarchs, Generals,
Delegates, Chairmen, take a large bowl, grease it, fill it
with flour and starch, butter and milk; add melted
chocolate chips into a crust brimming with syrup that
sticks to the palate, sweetens the tongue
and satisfies yearning without stuffing your pockets.
This recipe will not burst into flames.

Oh, sweet, sweet life that indulges the sugary urge,
licks lips, wipes a sticky mouth,
soothes the tongue with creams and coconut milk,
tickles the taste buds with peanut butter.
Oh lucky, lucky life in a world as delicious as mine.

Chapter 8

HOW THEY HAVE ENDURED THE HEAT

Naked Heat

It is hot.
Women in room 306 are nude;
all they wear are words,
words to be addressed on blank pages.
Breasts that dot i's, hold all u's close,
the way they caress others.

Breasts unencumbered tell tales.
Cleavage softens – finds freedom in a free fall.
Put your head against them,
feel the density, hear the beat,
listen to their stories,
how they love and live

how they have endured the heat.

Fragmented Woman

She is the foam
on ocean waves
fumbling up to shore
splattered
then sucked into the grains
of nature's foundation.

She is a mother's child
praying on the Sabbath
in frills and bows
and dishwater detergent.

She is the sweet virgin
of a father's dream
clouded in smoke
and the confusion
of mystical incense.

She is a devoted friend
whose hands are tied
at the sight of blood
and the smell of decay.

She is a confidante
of clowns,
on stage
in a tear speckled battlefield.

She is fragmented
torn at the seams
of connecting veins –
a concoction
of gurgling fluids,
drained and replenished,

split into pieces
then scattered
like raindrops
back to the sea.

Every Year We Hear Stories of Women
who walk on roads or avenues
as if they are free.
Some faces are open to the sun,
some partially covered in heat and wind,
some hidden by cloth
only their eyes are seen.
They move one foot in front of the other
only to go as far as man-made barricades,
clenched fists and open holy books allow.
They are forbidden passage,
fulfillment of their own dreams.
Beneath the cloth, the skirts, the jeans,
man's well-built chains hold tight.
Women broken and damaged
wait to be released,
wait for man's hand to set them free.
But man grips them by the throat,
throws them to the ground
and does all he can
to keep them there.

Some Girls on Another Planet
are born in slick, red rock formations,
taste water from splashing silver falls.
When they stand tall
they wash their tunics and rubber socks in the spray.

One sun stretches in its square box
across slow, slung clouds
exhaling crisp winds.

Trees turn in their sockets,
dig deep into molten, volcanic hills,
wide-veined leaves cling.

Birds and ants crawl into craters,
along the edge.
The young women tease them,
tap their tiny, feathered lips
with sticky girlish tongues and salted teeth.

They lick, bite, spray laughter
onto frightened creatures
whose small, wingless bodies
curl into circular shapes sweating fragrances
of white flowers and blue buds.

The girls cry at the sight, sneeze,
squeeze their nostrils shut.
White petals wriggle, secreting lavender scents.

As the double sun sets,
they wipe their tears,
nibble nervously at their mouths
and run off to return to their roots
partially overgrown in the dry, purple valley.

While We Are Asleep

While we are asleep a young woman
hangs herself in a bedroom
in her mother's house,
leaves a box of jewelry and a brief note.

As we turn restlessly toward the window,
a man stabs a neighborhood girl.
She screams and screams.
Everyone watches.

We cover ourselves in the chill with down quilts.
An old lady and her dog
huddle in the doorway of Ralph Lauren's store.
A sign says: "Everything on sale".

We wake from dreams of cruise ships,
cameras photograph a small child
holding his mother's hand as they float
lifeless in the ocean, under our very own moon.

We stiffen to cramps squeezing our legs
as lost people walk miles
in hostile lands,
then drop from fatigue.

While pillows fall to the floor during restless nights,
somewhere a woman is beaten,
a woman is raped,
a woman is stripped of her identity

and too often her life.

Home Alone

She enters, locks the door behind her.
Shades drawn, emptiness, silence,
stale New York air greets her.
Alone, she listens to her heartbeat.

With the flick of a switch shadows disappear.
She looks left to the oak table and four chairs.
A paisley shirt, not hers,
slouches on the wooden seat.
She tosses it into the trash,

touches the bookcase, smooth and white,
sets the paperbacks in line.
Her coat hangs in the closet
among empty hooks.

Cigarette butts sucked to death,
lay smashed in a glass ashtray.
For the last time she flushes them away.
Music of her choosing waltzes into the room.

She two-steps around the cushioned chair,
opens the window wide, lets the chill rush in.
She tap-toes into the kitchen to unfreeze a frozen dish
selected from her shopping list.

No beer, no bacon, no baked beans;
only fat-free milk, yogurt and
her very own Crispy Cream.

Fish or Foul

The ocean whined when fish were filed on slabs,
sold in the market place.
I wailed, sobbed that my own grandfather,
a real shark, I was told,
might be caught up in breadcrumbs
stuffed with crab.

I slept on an electric eel for stimulation.
Mother salted my tail until I became engaged
in trading options in the sea.
Green currency was battered on rocks
for small change.

I stood on the longest line
near a wall – all brick, gold and silicone implants.
The entrance to our country was small –-
like a thumb and forefinger touching.

Some scaled the wall with broken fins.
Guards armed with guns, knives and GMO'S
stood ready to lick their black crosses and kick ass.
We moved backwards, saluted left-handed.

No one could tell if we were coming or going.

Women's Work

to whiten laces wash them in sour milk
add a bit of cream for stiffness
sprinkle powder to soften hands
push and pull through zippers

for black laces use heated shoe polish
dip twice
save the juice

tend to this after beds are made
with spreads of 4200 threads
collect laundry wear purple plastic gloves
dump clothes at the bottom of basement steps
where the washer waits

soak dishes in orange juice pulp
place washed items on the dish drain
right side up
sip coffee until cold
add sugar for flavor and lipstick for color

dust wood furniture with old pajama bottoms
tear tops into small squares
dip in olive oil
polish what needs to shine

pin this to a white down pillow
beat the feathers out of it

What Is A Woman?
but soft hands
that touch tomorrow,
breath that sings into wind,
rain, the telephone?

She sees the feminine side of reality –
nourishment, peace, love.
She splits like flakes
as she frees herself from history's mantelpiece.

When time tightens its grip
extra hours fill her plate
with pits, rind, bitter spice
that she mixes and serves well.

Mascara darkens her lashes,
eyes dig deep for harmony.
Lipstick red as blood boils beneath
the apron, the bra, the powder puff.

Once her mission defined her
as the bimbo, the sexpot, property
but she squeezed through
the hourglass of time and broke the cast.

What is a woman if she cannot dance on nails
to her own tune or out of tune?
What is she but a slice of weather
raining over rutted roads she covers in linoleum?

And what are you, old woman,
but footprints left for me to follow?

Chapter 9

IF THIS THEN WHAT

Lungs

My lungs were hidden.
I never touched them, never saw them,
not even a thought about them.

As a child, I raced on Brooklyn streets,
ran as fast as I could.
Pounding in my chest slowed as I did.

My brother took me to neighborhoods,
to challenge the boys to a race. Even bet on me.
I raced down Lincoln Place ahead of them all.

At the seashore I swam, coasted waves,
belly-whopped until my lips turned blue,
until I heard my mother call.

One last dive under big waves.
I swallowed a mouthful of seawater,
tasted the salt, breathed in the foam.

In my teens, I watched with envy
as my mother smoked.
In films glamorous actresses exhaled

thick streams of smoke
through deep, red lips,
with poses full of desire and sex appeal.

I took my mother's cigarettes,
lit one up, breathed in deep,
blew out with a cool whistle shaped mouth.

Never wondered where the smoke went,
just blew it right out into the air.
In adult years, I lit one then another.

I was a woman who smoked in the morning,
walking to work, at work, after work. I puffed
before dinner, after, before bed, and upon waking.

I never thought about my lungs
until my lungs reprimanded me.

Wednesday, March 9th

I fell
on a city street,
missed the bus,
landed on my face,
my nose, my lip.
I lifted my head,
cupped my chin,
felt drops on my hands,
a hand on my shoulder.
Heard a woman's voice
on my right,
a man offered paper towels
another asked about calling 911.

As a senior I get:
half price Metrocards,
10% discount on Tuesdays
at D'Agostino's,
a price cut at movie theatres,
a seat on the train.
I wear flat shoes,
try hard to remember,
take calcium and vitamin D,
practice saying "What?" a lot.

I fell
fractured nose and sinuses,
my rite of passage-
I now declare myself Old.

Look at You, Old Tree

starting to bend.
Your bark has dried scales,
patches of dark and light.
Leaves that adorned
drop, decay on the hard earth.

Limbs are large and bruised.
Tender twigs broken, ailing,
twisted into arthritic shapes.
Thick branches hold firm,
some have had surgery
and near fatal accidents.
Struck hard by nature –
you suffer split wood, deep cuts.
Stormy days are rough.

Specialists bring gifts –
fertilizers, injections,
scores of knowing hands that treat
bark and bough, nests and fruit.
Fingers push against brawny elements
to heal, preserve, delay
the onslaught of rot at the root
or the death rattle of the saw.

If This, Then What

if the breath is colored blue
with white moist specks

if your mouth sucks in air
dusted with grey smoke

if the needle in your arm
cold intrusive piercing

if the lung puffs out
part of its lobe

if the black and white X-ray
shows scratches and tears

if the men in white coats
white pants and loafers

if the lights in the ceiling
bright unfiltered penetrate closed eyes

if the mask on your mouth feels light
your body chilled from a cold metal slab

if the slice from the left-hand corner
lifeless and skin-like

if the cigarette falls from
unsteady stained fingers

Breathe

The doctor calls
about the test,
the when and where.
I already know why.
There are new pains in my back
my legs and hands.
He will not be addressing that.
His specialty is lungs
lobes and mucous.

A needle is necessary to poke and pull
the uninvited white spot taking up residence
on the right, middle lobe.
Three lobes exist together –
inhaling, exhaling, clearing, clogging –
set in fluids, pipes, walls soft and thick.
I breathe in, breathe out.
All orchestrated before I knew the rules.

I Don't Want to Remember

The anesthesiologist wore a mask
across his nose and mouth
only his eyes visible.
I challenged him to prove who he was
He slid his covering down
revealed his face.
He held my hand
wrapped and punctured my arm.

    What did he look like?

The corridor was white, no, pale yellow
as I was driven on my back
on a cart with wheels.
Who was pushing me?
What happened to sound?
How did the walls open?

    I don't remember this route

Incoherent words hit me
like a slap.
What are they saying?
What do they want me to do?
Someone is counting
one, two, three lift.
I am hoisted through the air
onto white sheets.

    Where am I?

I am sleeping
with eyes partially shut,
a hard surface at my feet,
a bar I push with my toes.
I cannot lie flat on my back
the steel constricts me.
I try to sit up to move back-
stacks of pillows restrict me.
There is no way to rearrange them.
I am stuck in one place.

    I do not remember the bed.

Implements of different densities
press against me-
wires, plastic cups, remotes.
Wake up I tell myself
someone is here beside you.
My lips move, no sound.
Something is burning.
I try to turn away from it.
I am on fire.
Someone is putting it out.

    I don't remember who.

A nurse tells me not to move.
She grips my hand,
sticks a needle in my finger,
cups another with a thimble.
A thermometer is in my mouth,
a pulsing wrap around my arm.
Numbers flash on a monitor.
I realize I cannot turn over.

    I don't want to remember.

And When I Die

I just know
the big yoyo
in the sky
will pull me up
by my heart strings.

I have been spent
like a penny
in an odd year.

When I go
no one will know
they will be out to lunch
the way I spent my life –
without a tip.

I will smoke every cloud in sight
and if the surgeon general
discovers
it may cause life –
I will give it up
and practice my clarinet.

Once a cord got stuck
around my neck
they yanked and pulled
and called it birth.
I wonder if there is sickness after death.

In the Dark

on a dark day
I touch my beating heart
      feel it pulse

as I sense the wound
engraved down the middle of my life.

Imaginary blades weaken me
shed flesh and blood in my mind's eye.
      Strangers scrutinize me.

My head heavy as stones
cannot conjure up
      a white beach, a turquoise sea.

I fear the loss of my footprints.
Intensity from bright lights
      sets fire to panicky points of view.

Where are my people
who might cover my eyes,
      lift my head into a gentle position,

grease my dry lips, water my tongue,
speak words to soothe my psyche?

Help, I cry under my breath.
Those who answer are long dead,
      smiling, laughing, inviting me in.

Chapter 10

WE ARE DONE DOING OUR DUTY

We Are Done Doing Our Duty

We have done our duty –
walked the path of black and blue,
crammed our feet into high heels,
took big steps
through bushes and city streets.

We bowed when asked –
knelt in a river of fabrication
to reach the other side
where broken glass
reflected what would not be.

We changed our blouses and shirts –
covered up our underwear,
camouflaged ourselves
for the popular belief
of what should and shouldn't.

We read the writing on the wall
in elevators, bibles and law books,
stIffened at every lie,
spoke in whispers
with the hopes that someone heard.

We did what we were told –
wore appropriate styles,
recited words from universal texts
until our seams burst.

We Will Not

Get out, write words
that stop a clock,
war, women's pain.
Don't stop in fields
where bombs blast your syllables.
Give up punctuation
to swiftly convey
horrors of hunger.
Find a cause.
Loosen false fragments.
Speak out against atrocities.

We will not sit by
and watch freedom
be pricked by thorns,
deflated by our lack of words.
We will put sense on paper,
wood and bound books.
We will carve signs
into table tops that speak love.
We will not tear up our poems.
We will not take up silence
that suffocates.
We will not exhale an empty mind
or cut our thoughts into confetti.

Bureaucrats with their semicolons
in triplicate, memos to and from
revise policies without need for revision.
Those carbon copies
sit around oval tables in board rooms,
vote one after the other.
They provoke fires

that blaze around us
while they feign fear
in fireproof garb.
They try to force us
to live without our own words,
but we must not,
we cannot,
we will not.

Don't

Don't show me the right way to live.
Don't put your frame in my face.
Don't read me your holy books
about stoning and prison for loving like I do.
Your ancient laws were written by old men
when nights were lit with fire,
women were beasts of burden,
reproducing, serving the tribe
in tents that overflowed with taboos.
I don't want to know your bible
blessed the killing of a young Shepherd,
condoned the rape of a girl
for wearing trousers and a tie,
was silent when a man loved a man
and was beheaded for it.
Don't use your mumbo jumbo,
your churches, synagogues, and mosques
to write me off.
My body bends the same as yours.
Don't show me your electric prods
or tell me about "preference" –
do you believe I would choose
to swallow my feelings,
dance and love in dark alleys,
never speak my truth?
Don't tell me to feel at ease
when masses wish us dead,
laws degrade us,
gay teens take their lives to find peace.

Don't tell me how
Don't tell me who
Don't!

What We Should Fight Against

are voices that strike like lighting
citing bible passages that run red,
as cities burn.

What we should fight against
are books written by ancestors
with poison pens
shaping minds into patches
of worn out pockets.

What we should fight against
are forefathers who dictated
the source of feathers we must wear
and our children and our children's children.

What we should fight against
are words of hate,
branded skin, burning ovens
giving off lavender swirls of smoke –
identities squashed.

What we should fight against
are laws driven by religion
that has dust in its mouth,
frozen in a time when beheading
was entertainment.

What we should fight against
are rules rewritten by old men
in new suits, seated in their fathers' chairs
handing down their own commandments.

What we should fight against
are laws applauded in their time
then translated into ropes
tightly wound round our necks today.

Once

I stand tall now
in my own identity,
remember red rivers,
broken branches on thick trees,
women who taped their breasts flat,
rapes no one cared about.
I wear my own purple silk creation.
Shout out loud at parades
to those standing on sidelines,
to cameras that send my unveiled image
to my parent's home,
my co-workers at coffee breaks.
I sign my name
on lavender petitions
for freedom, for truth,
and in my own hand.

> *Still fear holds onto me,*
> *fear that my voice*
>
> *will find its way*
> *to an official black hole*
>
> *where cops, clergy, governments*
> *will cover me in their own cloth*
>
> *and force me*
> *to live beneath them again.*

2019: This Is Not the Time

Do we want to come out
while the President of the U.S.
is the main speaker at a
Hate Gay Rally.

His promises to end gay rights
are alarming –
no marriage, no jobs,
no places to congregate.

Boys with broken
crosses on their arms
will shed the blood
of dykes and queers.

Women who look like boys
and never wear lipstick
will be hanged again on thick branches
under city street lights.

Our families will reject us.
Friends will be dismissive
as if they never knew us,
never broke bread at our houses

where our dishes are washed,
our table set the same as theirs.
We want to be out,
feel free in our ordinary lives

but this is not the time.

What Does It Matter?

What does it matter what the lips form
when words spill out in odds and evens?

Someone is listening but not in this realm.
Are ears merely holes on the side of the head?

Who takes the smell from the rose buds
and leaves them empty of scent?

The cost of a dozen is not greater than
the passion of red; is it all about looks?

Do we strive to climb a steep mountain
or drop from heaven and work down from the top?

Who takes the love that you have to give
if it's wrapped in the wrong package?

Are all affections boxed up
waiting for someone to open them?

If you sneeze on the truth
who is responsible for its disinfectant?

 Can you scratch your head with one hand
while the other one waits and watches?

She read cards about spontaneity out slipped
the phrase "be yourself;" can you figure that out?

Do you want the ink to smear on this page
so, it will soak in and spoil all clarifications?

Silence

I

I am the silence
that smears a scarlet stain
across the apple tree.
I am the bite in the fruit
spat on the back of a serpent;
the dribble of juice flushed
from a woman's mouth
splashed into a naked man's eyes.
I am sacred words,
religious rhetoric
that bless some but not all.

I am pounded into stone walls,
stoned on fertile soil.
I am broken stained-glass windows,
a six-pointed star in yellow and lavender.
I am bent to the east.
My knees bleed onto gravel.
My head shaved, my robe, knotted.
I am cut between my legs,
scarred from obedience.

I am shame locked in an empty closet,
a criminal without a crime,
the butt of jokes,
tears in a mother's eyes,
the face battered by clenched hands.
I am the beaten woman
lying beside a woman.

I am a red bulb in a back room

casting shadows that never speak.
There is a stench of suicide and alcohol.
In this place tape binds the chest,
silk ties fit tightly
above a strand of pearls.
Everyone whispers.
Some give fake names.
A few wander in by mistake.

II

I am open now.
My steps firm,
oversized and thick with blisters.
I am beside you,
in front of you
and sometimes a few steps ahead.

I am lavender
in shirts and blouses,
pants, boots, open-toed shoes.
I am lyrics in songs,
a dancer in grand ballrooms.
I hold hands and dine out,
see role models
on the covers of magazines.

I shout into cities
from courts to roof tops,
alleyways to avenues,
farmhouses to fast-food chains.
I use a megaphone, a microphone
an Indian smoke signal.

I have found my voice.
Silence is no longer an option.

Joyce Jacobson grew up in Brooklyn, where she loved writing poetry, mostly by night, at her bedroom window. Her writing helped release tension and ease anxiety. Jacobson hid her poems in a brown leather folder, a gift given to her when she was seven years old by a young schoolboy who said he wanted to marry her. She still has the brown leather folder. She turned down his proposal.

Ms. Jacobson has an M.F.A from the New School for Social Research. She has lived most of her adult life in Manhattan. Her writing group of six women, formed from her membership in the International Women's Writing Guild, has been inspirational to her for many years. She now writes at a brightly lit desk or on a bench near the Hudson River.

www.ingramcontent.com/pod-product-compliance
Lightning Source LLC
Chambersburg PA
CBHW072151090426
42740CB00012B/2216